BEARS

Dagmar Fertl, Michelle Reddy &
Erik D. Stoops

Sterling Publishing Co., Inc.
New York

Edited and page design by Jeanette Green

Library of Congress Cataloging-in-Publication Data

Fertl, Dagmar.
    Bears / Dagmar Fertl, Michelle Reddy & Erik D. Stoops.
       p. cm.
    ISBN 0-8069-6541-X
       1. Bears—Juvenile literature. [1. Bears. 2. Questions and answers.] I. Reddy, Michelle.
    II. Stoops, Erik D., 1966– III. Title.
    QL 737.C27 F48 2000
    599.78—dc21   00-028509

                        1   3   5   7   9   10   8   6   4   2

                    Published by Sterling Publishing Company, Inc.
                        387 Park Avenue South, New York, N.Y. 10016
                    © 2000 by Dagmar Fertl, Michelle Reddy, and Erik D. Stoops
                            Distributed in Canada by Sterling Publishing
                    C/o Canadian Manda Group, One Atlantic Avenue, Suite 105
                                Toronto, Ontario, Canada M6K 3E7
                        Distributed in Great Britain and Europe by Chris Lloyd
                    463 Ashley Road, Parkstone, Poole, Dorset, BH14 0AX England
                    Distributed in Australia by Capricorn Link (Australia) Pty Ltd.
                    P. O. Box 6651, Baulkham Hills, Business Centre, NSW 2153, Australia
                                    Printed in Hong Kong

                                Sterling ISBN 0-8069-6541-X

Cover photo of polar bear by Richard Ellis. Photo of American black bear mother and cubs this page (above) by Pieter Folkens. Photos on Contents page opposite (p. 3): American Black Bear by Black Bear Conservation Committee; Asiatic Black Bear by International Fund for Animal Welfare, Chris Davis; Giant Panda by Grady Baxter; Spectacled Bear by Jennifer Warmbold; Polar Bear by Michelle Reddy; Brown Bear by Chicago Zoological Society, Mike Greer; Sloth Bear by Chicago Zoological Society, Howard Greenblatt; and Sun Bear by Chicago Zoological Society, Mike Greer.

CONTENTS

American Black Bear

Asiatic Black Bear

Giant Panda

Spectacled Bear

Polar Bear

Brown Bear

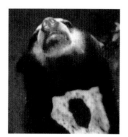

Sloth Bear

Sun Bear

GREAT BEARS
4

HOW BEARS LIVE
14

THE BEAR'S BODY
28

THE BEAR'S SENSES
38

EATING HABITS
44

BEAR REPRODUCTION
56

SELF-DEFENSE
64

BEARS AND PEOPLE
70

INDEX
80

GREAT BEARS

The Big Dipper, easy to find in the evening sky, is in the constellation Ursa Major, or the "Great Bear."

Bears are inquisitive, strong, and fast. Bears are the largest and one of the strongest carnivores on land.

Their ancestors are an offshoot of the ancient Canidae family of dogs, wolves, foxes, and coyotes.

Photo by Chicago Zoological Society, Mike Greer

▲ *Polar bears are the largest of the bears.*

How many different kinds of bear are there?

Eight different kinds or species of bear live on Earth today. Each species has differences in size, color, and other adaptations that help them survive in their particular habitat.

The weight of bears varies greatly, depending on things such as population, habitat, food availability, weather, and season.

Opposite. Photo of brown bears play-fighting by Chicago Zoological Society, Mike Greer

Which bear species is the largest?

The POLAR BEAR (*Ursus maritimus*) is the largest bear species, and it is the only bear species that's a marine mammal.

Males weigh from 770 to 1,430 pounds (350–650 kg), but one very large polar bear weighed 2,210 pounds (1,002 kg). Females can weigh from 330 to 550 pounds (150–250 kg).

We think of polar bears as being white, but their coats actually range in color from ivory to pale tan. In a zoo, you sometimes see a polar bear that appears to be green. This is from green algae growing in the hollow hair shafts of a polar bear's coat.

Underneath its heavy fur coat, the polar bear's skin is black. This helps absorb heat from the sun.

How many different kinds of brown bear are there?

Using DNA, scientists have found only one species of BROWN BEAR (*Ursus arctos*), with several subspecies like the grizzly and the Kodiak.

All are large bears, but they vary in size, depending on where they live and what they eat. Bears that live near the ocean and eat salmon can weigh twice as much as inland bears.

The Alaskan Kodiak, which gorges itself on salmon, can weigh up to 1,700 pounds (773 kg). Kodiak bears can even grow to be larger than polar bears.

◀ *Left and above left.* *While some individual brown bears may grow to be larger than polar bears, on the average, the polar bear species is larger.*

Photo by Michelle Reddy

Photo by Chicago Zoological Society, Mike Greer

◀ *Far left.* *Adult male brown bears usually weigh from 330 to 825 pounds (150–375 kg). Females weigh about half as much as males.*

◀ *Near left.* *Kodiak bears have a light ring of fur around the neck.*

What bear is named for eyeglasses?

The SPECTACLED BEAR (*Tremarctos ornatus*) is a medium-size bear. It is 175 to 275 pounds (80–125 kg) and gets its name from the white- to gold-colored rings of fur around its eyes.

These rings make the bear look like it is wearing eyeglasses or spectacles.

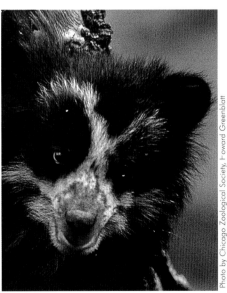

Photo by Chicago Zoological Society, Mike Greer

Photo by Chicago Zoological Society, Foward Greenblatt

▲ *Each spectacled bear has a different eye-ring pattern that helps us tell them apart.*

Obviously, black bears are black...right?

The medium-size AMERICAN BLACK BEAR (*Ursus americanus*) isn't always black. These bears can also be dark brown, cinnamon, blue, grayish blue, silvery gray, reddish yellow, orange, pale cream, or blond.

One variation of the black bear is white! The blue or glacier bear is a rare sight.

▲ *Depending on the season, male black bears can weigh from 125 to 600 pounds (57–273 kg). Female black bears are smaller.*

If a black bear can be brown, how can you tell it apart from a real brown bear?

It can be hard to tell the difference between a brown American black bear and its cousin the brown bear.

Look for these clues: The brown bear has a hump between its shoulders, longer claws than a black bear, and a dish-shaped face.

If it's in a tree, most likely you've found a black bear. You be the detective!

▲ *The name* grizzly bear *refers to the silver-tipped or grizzled hair of this brown bear.*
You can also see the distinct shoulder hump of the brown bear.

Photo Reno P. Sommerhalder

▲ *White-haired black bears are not albinos. They have a limited range in British Columbia, where they are about as common as red-haired people (one in ten).*
This bear is known as the Kermode, ghost, or spirit bear.

Are all commonly named black bears found in America?

No. There is another species of black bear called the ASIATIC BLACK BEAR (*Ursus thibetanus*). Bet you can guess where it lives!

Asiatic black bears are medium-size bears, slightly smaller than some of their North American cousins. The weight varies from 220 to 440 pounds (100–200 kg) for males and from 110 to 275 pounds (50–125 kg) for females.

Generally, the black fur of the Asiatic black bear is longest around its shoulders and neck.

Photo by Pieter Folkens

◀ *Brown-colored black bears range in color from light cinnamon to dark chocolate, which can cause people to confuse this bear with a brown bear.*

▶ *The Asiatic black bear is sometimes called a moon bear because of the white crescent on its chest.*

Photo by International Fund for Animal Welfare, Chris Davis

Which bear is the most unusual?

The SLOTH BEAR (*Melursus ursinus*) is one of the most unusual-looking bears. It is medium-size. Males weigh from 175 to 320 pounds (80–145 kg), and females are just a bit smaller at 120 to 210 pounds (55–95 kg).

They tend to be black with a ruff of fur around the neck, white or yellowish chest markings, and a long grayish muzzle covered with very little hair. Sloth bears can be dangerous, especially if startled.

▲ *The sloth bear was once thought to be a bearlike sloth. We know better now.*

▲ *Adult male giant pandas weigh 175 to 275 pounds (80–125 kg), about 10 to 20% more than adult females.*

Which bear was once thought to be related to the raccoon?

For many years, people thought that the GIANT PANDA (*Ailuropoda melanoleuca*) was not a bear at all, but a relative of the raccoon.

Scientists now tell us that DNA evidence shows that giant pandas are really and truly bears.

Of all the bear species, which is the smallest?

The SUN BEAR (*Helarctos malayanus*) is the smallest of the bears. It is about the size of a large dog!

Sun bears get their name from a blond chest patch of fur that looks like a setting sun and stands out against their black fur.

The average male sun bear weighs about 60 to 145 pounds (27–65 kg), and the average female weighs about 100 pounds (45 kg).

Photo by Michelle Reddy

▲ *Sun bears are also known as honey bears because they really like the sweet, sticky stuff.*

11

▲ *Koalas are related to kangaroos because both species carry young in a pouch.*

There are seven levels of classification: kingdom, phylum, class, order, family, genus, species. The largest is the kingdom. Let's use the example of an animal. Animals belong to the animal kingdom.

The animal kingdom is broken down into smaller groups of animals, called phyla, that are similar. For example, Chordata includes all animals with backbones. Each level of classification gets smaller and smaller until there is just one kind of animal.

For example, all bears are in the same family, Ursidae; the ones that are most alike (polar, brown, American black, and Asiatic black) are in the same genus, *Ursus*, but each one is a separate species.

Each type of animal has two parts to its name. The first word is the genus and the second is the species. An example is *Ursus arctos*, the brown bear's scientific name.

That's eight. But didn't you forget about koala bears?

No, we didn't. Even though they are sometimes called koala bears, koalas are actually not bears at all. Because the female carries her young in a pouch, koalas belong to an order of mammals called Marsupialia, or marsupials.

How do scientists classify bears?

To help identify and name living things, scientists called taxonomists developed a naming system (using Latin) that groups living things by how they are alike and different.

People all over the world use these scientific names.

Scientific Classification

Here is the classification scheme for brown bears.

KINGDOM **Animalia** The word animalia means "animal."

PHYLUM **Chordata** Chordata include vertebrates—animals with backbones.

CLASS **Mammalia** Mammals are warm-blooded, have hair, breathe air with lungs, give birth to live young, and nurse their young with milk from mammary glands.

ORDER **Carnivora** These are carnivores—animals that can eat meat.

FAMILY **Ursidae** This is the Latin word for the bear family.

GENUS *Ursus* This is the genus for brown, polar, American black, and Asiatic black bears.

SPECIES *arctos* This is the species for brown bears.

Are there any extinct bears?

Yes. Two you may have heard about are the CAVE BEAR (*Ursus speleaus*) and the GIANT SHORT-FACED BEAR (*Arctodus simus*), which have been extinct for a long time.

Today's spectacled bear is a direct descendant of the short-faced bear, which was the largest carnivore of the last ice age.

▲ *Genus and species.* People all over the world can identify the brown bear by its scientific name, Ursus arctos.

HOW BEARS LIVE

Of the eight bear species that live on Earth, four live in the Southern Hemisphere and four in the Northern Hemisphere. Bears in the Northern Hemisphere are found in temperate forests and the Arctic.

Which bears live where? Do bears hang out in groups? What does a bear den look like?

◀ *Opposite page.* Like all animals, bears need to live near food and water. This American black bear lives near an Alaskan salmon run.

Photo by Pieter Folkens

▶ *Near and far right.* Spectacled bears are the only wild bears living in South America. They feed and rest in trees in the cool, wet, cloud forests high in the Andes Mountains of Bolivia, Peru, Ecuador, Colombia, and Venezuela.

Where in the world do bears live?

Wild bears live in environments that range from hot and humid tropics to the bitterly cold Arctic.

North America is home to three of the world's eight bear species—brown, American black, and polar bears. Almost two-thirds of the bears in the world live in North America.

Bears probably originated in China, where four species still live—giant panda, brown, Asiatic black, and sun bears.

Photo by Jennifer Warmbold

Photo by Reno P. Sommerhalder

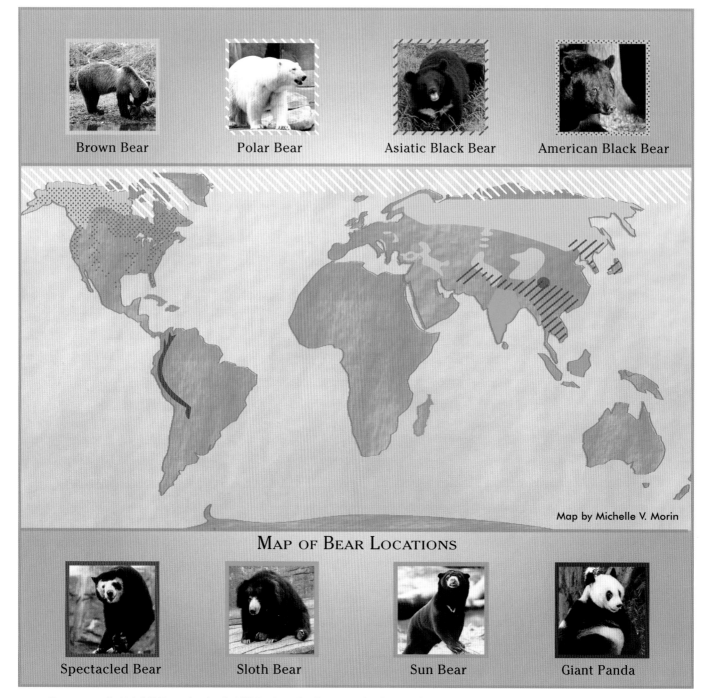

Brown Bear

Polar Bear

Asiatic Black Bear

American Black Bear

MAP OF BEAR LOCATIONS

Map by Michelle V. Morin

Spectacled Bear

Sloth Bear

Sun Bear

Giant Panda

This map, created by Michelle V. Morin, is based on the IUCN Bear Action Plan. Photos: Brown bear by Pieter Folkens; polar bear by Chicago Zoological Society, Mike Greer; Asiatic black bear by International Fund for Animal Welfare, Chris Davis; American black bear by Black Bear Conservation Committee; spectacled bear by Jennifer Warmbold; sloth bear by Chicago Zoological Society, Mike Greer; sun bear by Jennifer Warmbold; and giant panda by Michelle Reddy.

Where do polar bears live?

About 21,000 to 28,000 polar bears live in the Arctic, including parts of Alaska, northern Canada, Russia, Greenland, and Norway.

They are found on sea ice, water, and islands—anywhere the water meets the shore and ice continually freezes and thaws.

Do any polar bears live at the North Pole?

Polar-bear tracks have been found almost at the North Pole.

Usually polar bears do not venture so far north, since the northern Arctic Ocean has little food for them.

▲ *You would never see polar bears* (left) *and penguins* (right) *side by side. That's because polar bears live well north of the Equator in the Arctic, and penguins, like these king penguins, live only south of the Equator.*

▲ *Black bears keep to wooded areas, making it hard for us to see them.*

Where are brown bears found?

Brown bears once lived throughout Europe, western North America, much of Asia, and on the Arctic tundra.

Less than 200,000 brown bears are left in the world. Most live in Asia and North America, but small populations still survive in many European countries.

Which bear is the most common?

The brown bear is the most widely distributed bear in the world.

However, there are more American black bears than any other type of bear.

Where are American black bears found?

American black bears are found in North America.

They live in much of Canada, the United States, and even in the Sierra Madres south into Mexico.

▲ *Brown bears live in dense forests, alpine tundra, and river valleys of North America, Europe, and Asia. They often move into treeless open areas, which makes them more visible than American black bears.*

Photo by Michelle Reddy

Photo by Cliff Rice

▲ Giant pandas live in cool, damp bamboo forests high in the mountains of inland China.

They depend on these forests for food, since they feed on bamboo shoots. But these bamboo forests are shrinking. Giant pandas now survive in only six small areas and are seriously endangered.

▲ Sloth bears live in a variety of habitats, including thorn forests and wet tropics. These bears are found in Sri Lanka, India, Bhutan, and Bangladesh.

▶ Asiatic black bears live in hilly or mountainous country with brush and forest.

These bears are found throughout Asia: Pakistan, Afghanistan, Russia, Tajikistan, China, India, Bhutan, Nepal, Thailand, Cambodia, Vietnam, Laos, Myanmar (Burma), Japan, Korea, and Taiwan.

Photo by International Fund for Animal Welfare, Chris Davis

Photo by Michelle Reddy

▲ Sun bears live in dense tropical rain forests of southeast Asia. Their range is from Bangladesh east to Vietnam and south to the Malay Peninsula and the islands of Sumatra and Borneo.

19

Do bears live in groups?

Bears are loners, except where food is concentrated.

You may see many bears at streams when salmon swim from the ocean back up rivers to spawn.

Several bears may be at berry patches, trash dumps, and near large numbers of insects. When polar bears are on land, because of changes in the ice, bears may be together.

Males and females are together for only a few days during mating season. Only females with their cubs stay together through the year.

▼ *Bears are not usually social. These brown bears at a salmon run tolerate each other because of the abundant food.*

Can you see the three brown bears in this photo?

Photo by Hans-Joachim Muench

Who's the boss?

Bears are usually found alone. If bears come together, a certain order occurs, with a boss. For example, adult males are at the top (most dominant) and cubs are at the bottom. Adult females and juvenile bears fall somewhere in the middle.

Adult females fiercely defend their cubs and food resources against male bears.

Photo by Reno P. Sommerhalder

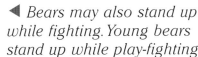

Photo by Irene Rathburn

▲ *Bears stand up to look around, reach food, mark trees, fight, or play. This mother bear, protecting her cubs, stands up to check for danger and for other bears.*

Standing on hind legs helps the bear "sniff the air." Standing up is usually not a threatening pose.

◀ *Bears may also stand up while fighting. Young bears stand up while play-fighting.*

21

Photo by Bernie Peyton

▲ *Spectacled bears in South America made the claw marks on this cactus.*

Photo by Reno P. Sommerhalder

▲ *You may see bear hair along the routes bears travel. Bears rub against trees, which leaves hair and an odor, to leave messages for each other.*

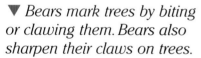

▼ *Bears mark trees by biting or clawing them. Bears also sharpen their claws on trees.*

▼ *This tree, marked by bears' clawing and chewing on it, tells us that grizzlies are in the area.*

Photo by Reno P. Sommerhalder

Photo by Adolph Murie

How do bears "talk" to each other?

One way bears communicate is with body language, or how they move the head, ears, mouth, and body. Bears also communicate with sound; for example, spectacled bears trill to their cubs.

Another way is by using scents—odor from hair, urine, and feces. When bears rub against trees or urinate along a trail, the scent left behind may tell other animals that they are in the area.

Why do bears bite and claw trees?

Bears pick certain trees along their trails and make deep scratches with their claws. The same tree may have old and new marks. When bears rub against them, they may leave hairs in these scratches, especially when shedding a winter coat.

We do not know why bears do this. It may be another way of telling other animals who is in the neighborhood.

What kind of sounds do bears make?

Bears make all sorts of sounds. They roar, grunt, trill, huff, pop teeth, and snort. Cubs may hum when they're nursing, and they whine or bawl when they are upset or scared. A mother may grunt and make other sounds to tell cubs to climb a tree, get out of danger, or come to her side.

How long do bears live?

A 30-year-old bear is an old-timer. You can tell the age of a bear by its teeth.

Take a thin piece of a tooth, stain it with a special dye, and count its layers, just as you would count the growth rings in a tree. The number of layers gives the bear's age.

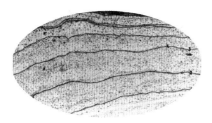

▲ *This is a cross section of a bear's tooth. This bear is 8 years old. Each year is marked as a new layer in the tooth.*

▲ *The closest relatives of bears are seals, sea lions, and walruses. These are California sea lions that have hauled out of the ocean.*

What are the ancestors of bears?

Bears are descended from small, insect-eating mammals called miacids (pronounced "my-E-sids"), which lived during the time of the dinosaurs.

About 30 to 40 million years ago, in the Oligocene epoch, some of these insect eaters began evolving into bears. The first true bears evolved from heavy bearlike dogs during the Oligocene, some 27 million years ago.

The oldest known bear—the DAWN BEAR—is about 20 million years old and was the size of a small dog.

Did bears ever live in Africa, Australia, or Antarctica?

Bears have never lived in Australia or Antarctica, but fossils of bears have been found in Africa. We don't know why bears do not live in Africa today.

23

▲ *A female black bear with cubs may den in a brush pile like this.*

What is a den?

A den is a safe place to avoid very cold weather, to hibernate, and to give birth.

A den can be a hole in the ground, in a snowdrift, or in the base of a tree. It could be a cavity high up in a tree trunk, even when surrounded by water, or just a nest of grasses built on the ground or against an overturned tree root.

Some bears use the same den year after year; others make a new one every year.

▲ *A black bear, like this large male lying in a grass nest, may den in unsheltered beds.*

▲ *A black bear den can be inside a hollow tree at ground level or high aboveground, or in a cave, or under a fallen tree, or in an unsheltered bed.*

Do all bears use dens?

No, it depends on the abundance of food and the bear species. Cold winter weather, lack of food, and giving birth drive bears to use dens.

American black, Asiatic black, and brown bears all den for the winter—both male and female—and have young in the den. However, where the food supply is plentiful year-round, members of even these species may not den.

Some Kodiak bears (brown bears), for example, have been known to eat salmon all winter. In Yosemite, some black bears stayed out of dens in years when acorn crops were plentiful.

Black bears in Florida do not den. Brown and Asiatic black bears living in mild climates also may not den.

Normally, only female polar bears use dens. But when the weather is bad or seals are hard to find, males sometimes use snow dens. They stay for a few days or weeks to conserve energy.

Photo by Minnesota Department of Natural Resources, Pam Coy

▲ *Bedding in a den can be grasses, leaves, pine needles, bamboo shoots, and tree branches. Bedding is about 7 to 9 inches (18–23 cm) deep.*

We don't know how much other bear species use dens, but we do know that female sloth bears, sun bears, and giant pandas give birth in dens.

Photo by Reno P. Sommerhalder

▶ *Brown bears have dens under large boulders or dug into hillside slopes.*
A hillside den traps heat nicely. When snow covers the den, it provides more insulation against the cold.

Where do bears sleep?

Some bears, like American black bears, Asiatic black bears, and spectacled bears, may sleep in trees. Sometimes Asiatic black bears and spectacled bears make "nests" in trees and even sit on them while they eat.

Other bears sleep in shallow holes in the ground, rock crevices, or at the foot of a tree. American black bears seem to find a comfortable place to lie down. In cool weather, they curl up, and when it is hot, they lie on the back with their feet in the air. Polar bears dig pits in the snow.

Do American black bears have territories?

A bear may travel many miles (kilometers) in a day looking for food. Where a bear spends time, finds food and water, and sleeps is its home range. The home range of one bear sometimes overlaps another bear's.

Bears sometimes fight to protect a food patch, like a berry bush or animal carcass.

▲ *Bears pick places to live that are near water. Bears need water to survive, and they use water to cool off and escape insects.*

Females are territorial, favoring specific areas. Males are larger and need more food and larger ranges. Males roam and try to mate with as many females as possible. A female bear has a smaller range because she takes care of cubs and cannot travel as far with them.

When the cubs leave their mom, a young female usually occupies a small area within her mother's home range. By the time she is mature and ready to have her own cubs, she pretty much has her own territory.

▲ *Bears often use the same path to visit a food source or travel through their home area. Over time, they establish a trail. This is a bear trail through a meadow of cow parsnip, a plant that bears eat.*

When are bears most active?

Most bear species are active in the daytime. Sloth bears are the only bears more active at night, perhaps to avoid the heat. That's also probably why most bears rest in the middle of the day but feed and move about in the morning, late afternoon, or evening.

Bears change their habits to avoid danger during their normal active time. Around campgrounds or places with lots of people, black and brown bears become more nocturnal to avoid human activity. At salmon streams and garbage dumps, young bears and females with cubs feed during midday or late at night to avoid big, dominant bears that feed in the evening.

Unlike other sloth bears, female sloth bears with young are more active during the day. This probably helps them avoid large, male sloth bears and other predators that hunt at night.

▶ *This grizzly is scratching an itch on an old drain pipe.*

▲ *Polar bears clean themselves after eating seals, since seal fat is very greasy. Clean hair keeps polar bears insulated against the cold. Polar bears use water or rub themselves in the snow.*

Do bears take baths?

Bears swim, bathe in water, scratch and lick themselves, and rub against rocks or in grass. Bears that live in cold areas are especially careful about grooming, since clean hair means a warm fur coat.

Are bears smart?

Yes. People consider bears smart. Bears learn quickly and are curious. They have good memories about where to locate food, and they find creative ways to solve and avoid problems.

THE BEAR'S BODY

Generally, bears have a large, fur-covered body; a big head with small, rounded ears; a short tail; and stout, strong legs.

Each bear species has minor variations of this general body plan that are adaptations to help it survive in its particular habitat.

Some bears are better at climbing, while others are better at swimming or running.

Look carefully at the body of each species to see clues that show what it does best and where it lives.

▲ *When it's too warm, a polar bear cools down by panting like a dog or lying on its belly on wet dirt or ice. Bears lose most of their heat from their paws.*

Which are larger, male or female bears?

As adults, male bears are larger than females of the same species.

Why are some types of bear big while others are small?

The larger a bear's body, the more heat it can hold. When a large pie and a small pie are taken hot from the oven, the large pie takes longer to cool. That's because its large size helps hold the heat better.

Bears in cold temperatures need to hold heat. Polar bears are so well adapted to Arctic cold that they need to cool down when it is warm.

◄ *Opposite page. A brown bear reflects on a watering hole.*

Is size the only thing that keeps bears warm?

No. Bears also have a layer of fat that acts like a wetsuit to keep heat inside the body. This fat layer may be up to 4½ inches (11 cm) thick. In bitter cold, a polar bear may bury iteself in snow, which helps insulate it from the weather.

Some bears go into a deep sleep during the coldest time of year. This helps them escape the shortage of food brought on by cold weather.

That's called hibernation, right?

Basically, yes. Scientists have debated about what hibernation means. During hibernation, an animal's breathing and heart rate drops, and its body cools down.

This change is not as drastic in bears as in some other animals. Bears can also be awakened fairly easily. Ground squirrels, sometimes called "true hibernators," cannot. But during hibernation, which can last for 1 to 5 months, the bear's body does some pretty amazing things.

▲ *Bears, like this spectacled bear, do not have to be in a deep sleep to snore.*

▲ *Most brown bears hibernate. But some that live in places where food is available throughout the year do not hibernate.*

▲ *Polar bears have a thick coat with 9,677 hairs per square inch (1,500 per sq cm). If kept clean, the polar bear's thick coat insulates it from icy water and frigid air.*

During hibernation, the bear can live off its body fat and doesn't need to eat or drink anything. It doesn't defecate either. Its body can somehow recycle body waste into protein—something scientists still don't understand. During hibernation, bears only need about half the oxygen they normally do.

But not all bears hibernate, and some that usually do may skip hibernating if the food supply is good.

Generally, bears that hibernate live in temperate or polar regions. Asiatic black bears, American black bears, some brown bear subspecies, and pregnant polar bears hibernate.

When they wake up, they may have lost 15 to 25% or more of their weight. It is important for bears to fatten up before they hibernate. Maybe this is why we say "hungry as a bear."

Doesn't the fur coat keep them warm, too?

That's right. All bears have a thick coat of fur that they shed every year. This coat has long outer guard hairs and fine, thick underfur. Guard hairs protect the underfur, which insulates the bear and keeps out the cold—but only if it is kept well groomed.

This coat can also help a bear stay cool in warm temperatures. It keeps out heat, acts as a raincoat to keep the bear dry, protects the skin from cuts and scrapes, and keeps out biting insects. The sun bear has the shortest coat of all bears.

▲ *Sloth bears live in warm places where they can find food year-round, so they don't need to hibernate.*

▲ *The giant panda's slightly oily fur repels raindrops and makes an ideal raincoat.*

I've heard that polar-bear hairs are hollow. Sunlight passes through the hair shafts reflecting from side to side, until heat is generated to warm the bear. True?

Great story, right? Actually, this is not true. But it is true that polar bears have hollow guard hairs, just like the hair of many arctic mammals. Sunlight can pass through the hollow hairs and the bear's black skin absorbs the heat.

▶ *An electron microscope shows the hollow hair of a polar bear.*

Are bears born with fur?

No. Most bears are born without fur. Only polar bears and giant pandas are born with thin white fur.

▶ *The lips of bears, like those of this sloth bear, are not attached to their gums. This makes them look rubbery.*

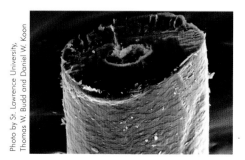

What do their teeth look like?

Because bears are omnivores, they have teeth that allow them to eat both plants and meat. Broad, flat molars are great for grinding plant food. The large canines and incisors can be used for self-defense and to catch, kill, and tear prey. Most bears have 42 teeth. That's ten more than people have!

Sloth bears do not have two front incisors. This helps them make a tube with the mouth to suck up termites and ants, their main food.

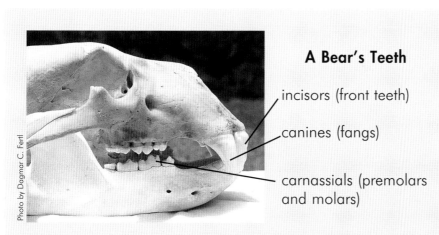

A Bear's Teeth

incisors (front teeth)

canines (fangs)

carnassials (premolars and molars)

Bears are in the order Carnivora. All animals in this order have carnassial teeth. The carnassials are especially designed to slice and cut off meat.

▲ *Bears, like this brown bear, use their teeth to eat and to protect themselves.*

▲ *More than 99% of a giant panda's diet is made up of bamboo stems and leaves.*
 That's why a giant panda's molars are wider and flatter than those of other bears.

Are bears strong?

Bears are very powerful. They can move objects that weigh much more than they do.

▲ *A brown bear may move a ton of rocks and dirt while building a den.*

What are their feet like?

Bears have large paws with five toes, each with an unretractable claw. Claws on the front paws are longer than claws on the back.

Claws are handy for lots of things like climbing, running, digging, catching fish, and self-defense.

▶ *Paw prints show a brown bear sow (large, on the left) walking with her cub (small, on the right).*
Compare the size of the bear prints with the human footprint in the upper left.

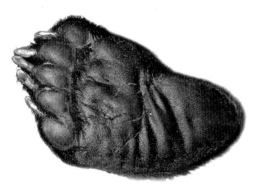

Photo by Chicago Zoological Society, Jim Schulz

▲ *Most bears tend not to have hair on the bottoms of their feet. This paw belongs to a brown bear.*

34

Photo by Bill Applegate

Which bear has the best feet?

Each bear species has the best feet for where it lives and how it uses its feet.

Polar bears have amphibious feet that make good snowshoes for walking in deep snow and perfect paddles for swimming. They are very wide (12 inches or 30 cm) and partially webbed. Their sharp, hooked claws give them good traction on ice.

Most bears have bare feet, but polar bear paws have fur on the bottoms and between the toes. This helps keep the feet warm and helps prevent them from slipping on ice.

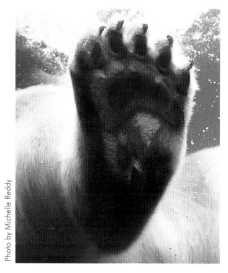

▲ *While most bears have bare feet, the paws of polar bears have fur on the bottoms and between the toes.*

▲ *Bears have nonretractable claws, like dogs and unlike cats. Claws give them traction for climbing and running. They are also good for digging.*

How do they walk?

Like people, bears walk by putting their feet flat on the ground. This kind of walking is called plantigrade (pronounced "PLAN-ti-grade"). Also, bears can stand on their hind legs and use their front legs for fighting or reaching into trees.

Giant pandas are a little bit different because they lack a heel pad. They are not completely plantigrade. When they stand or walk, their heels do not touch the ground.

▲ *The owner of these feet is a spectacled bear. Notice the bare feet and the longer claws of the front paws.*

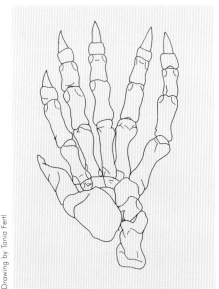

Drawing by Tania Ferl

Photo by Michelle Reddy

▲ *Giant pandas have a large wrist bone that forms a sixth digit or "thumb." This helps them grasp bamboo stems.*

Why are bears pigeon-toed?

Tree-climbing bears tend to be pigeon-toed or bow-legged in the front. This helps them "hug" the tree while they climb. It also allows them to use their forelegs as "hands"— for scooping, grabbing, and bringing food to the mouth.

▶ *This spectacled bear is pacing. Notice how the front and rear legs of each side move together when the bear walks. Bears sometimes walk like this.*

Photo by Chicago Zoological Society, Howard Greenblatt

▲ *Because bears are plantigrade, they can stand on their hind feet and even walk upright. These are polar bears.*

Photo by Michelle Reddy

Polar bears are also too large to climb trees, and not many trees grow in the Arctic where they live.

Who gets the gold medal for running?

Over short distances, polar bears and brown bears can run about 30 to 35 mph (56 km).

Are bears good swimmers?

All bears are good swimmers, but the gold medal goes to the polar bear.

Polar bears can swim up to 4 to 6 mph (6 to 10 km/hr) for 100 miles (161 km). They use their paws as paddles. One polar bear swam 200 miles (322 km) without stopping!

When swimming, they close their nostrils and flatten their ears against the head to keep out water. Polar bears are also very good underwater swimmers.

▲ *Even though brown bears do not climb trees as adults, they are still pigeon-toed.*

Can all bears climb trees?

Asiatic and American black bears, giant pandas, sloth bears, and spectacled bears are great climbers, but sun bears may be the best of all.

Brown bears are too large as adults to climb trees; however, as cubs, they can climb trees for protection.

▲ *Polar bears are great swimmers, both underwater...*
▼ *...and at the surface.*

THE BEAR'S SENSES

The five senses are hearing, sight, smell, taste, and touch.

Senses are important. They help animals learn about their environment, locate a mate, and avoid danger. They help them identify their mother or offspring and find a good dinner.

Bears see almost as well as we do. Their hearing is a little better, but their ability to smell is far better than ours.

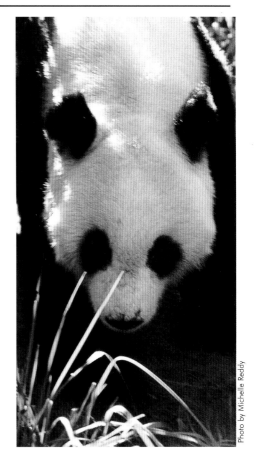

Photo by Michelle Reddy

◀ *Page opposite. This brown bear is scratching its chest on a rock bed in an Alaskan stream in summer.*

Like most animals, bears sometimes have to find creative ways to scratch an itch.

Photo by Reno P. Sommerhalder

What is a bear's best sense?

By far, a bear's best sense is smell—some people even call them "noses with legs." They are among the best smellers on Earth.

Polar bears can track down an odor from 20 miles (32 km) away, and they can even smell a dead seal under 20 feet (6 m) of snow.

Why do bears move their ears?

Many animals move their ears (or pinnae) to pick up and locate sounds. When you are big, it takes a whole lot less energy to move your ears than it does to move your whole body.

The only bear species that does not move its ears is the giant panda.

▲ *Like other bears, giant pandas have an acute sense of smell.*

Bears communicate with each other by leaving scent marks on trees, plants, and snow. With scent marks, a female bear tells male bears she is ready to breed. A male bear identifies its territory.

▲ *Bears, like this sun bear, may be able to hear sounds too high for human ears.*

▲ *"My! What big ears you have!" Some people think the American black bear has the largest ears of all bear species.*

Which bear species has the largest ears?

Some people think that the American black bear has the biggest ears, but others believe the Asiatic black bear's ears are larger.

The sloth bear definitely has the hairiest of them all.

◀ *Bears, like this Asiatic black bear, use their senses to help them survive.*

▲ *A fancy name for the part of the ear that we see is* pinna (pinnae *is the plural*). *The cup-shaped pinna helps direct sound into the ear canal.*

Can bears see well?

That depends on what you mean by well. Bears may not see details at a distance very well, but they have good depth perception and good peripheral (along-the-side) vision.

They can even see colors. They are also able to detect movement from far away.

If you came upon a bear in the wild, it might not see you if you stood still. If you were downwind, the bear could not smell you. However, if you moved, the bear might discover you.

▲ *Black bears are able to see colors, which helps them recognize edible plants, nuts, and fruits like these blueberries.*

▲ *Polar bears see well both above and below water.*

▶ *The polar bear's third eyelid helps protect it from getting snow blindness from the bright light that reflects off snow.*

What does a giant panda have in common with many nocturnal animals?

As in many nocturnal animals, the pupil of the giant panda's eye is a vertical slit.

▲ *Giant pandas can see both by day and at night.*

Do bears have eyelids?

They actually have three. Like people, they have top and bottom eyelids. They also have a third one called a nictitating membrane.

This thin, clear eyelid protects the eyes from getting scratched and being exposed to light that is too bright. It also has a special secretion that helps prevent the eye from drying out.

Do bears taste well?

Generally, for land animals, the sense of smell is related to the sense of taste.

So, scientists think that because bears have a good sense of smell, they must have a good sense of taste, too.

▶ *This sun bear demonstrates use of its very long tongue. The tongue not only helps taste food but also helps extract food from tight places.*

Photo by Jennifer Warmbold

Photo by Chicago Zoological Society, Howard Greenblatt

▲ *The sloth bear's long, shaggy coat prevents ants and termites from reaching the bear's more sensitive skin.*

If bears are covered with hair, can they feel anything?

Believe it or not, hair as well as skin can be sensitive to touch. The hair and whiskers of bears are rooted in the skin, where they are connected to sense organs.

This allows a bear to "feel" with its whiskers and other hair. Bears also feel with their skin. Their feet and nose are particularly sensitive.

▶ *When a bear wants to touch something, it may put its nose close and move its whiskers forward to sense the item.*

Photo by Chicago Zoological Society, Mike Greer

EATING HABITS

Bears are often called carnivores, which means "animals that can eat meat."

You might be surprised to know that most bears are actually omnivores. They eat mostly berries, nuts, roots, and insects.

What different kinds of food do bears like to eat?

How do they find and catch their food?

Photo by Reno P. Sommerhalder

▲ *Brown and black bears in Alaska feed on a variety of fruits and plants, including salmonberries, blueberries, huckleberries, wild strawberries, and fireweed flowers.*

What do bears eat?

Bears eat mainly fruit, plants, and insects. They're omnivores. *Omnivores,* like bears and people, can eat both animals and plants.

Bears are opportunists and take advantage of whatever food they find. Most bears will eat meat if they can get it.

What do polar bears eat?

Polar bears eat seals and scavenge walrus and whale carcasses. The bear's favorite part of the seal is the fat.

During the summer, when the ice melts and polar bears are on land, they sometimes eat birds, eggs, vegetation, and small mammals like lemmings.

They may even rummage through people's garbage if they venture inland.

◀ *Opposite page.* *Giant pandas mainly eat bamboo—about 30 pounds (13.5 kg) a day! If they get a chance, they will also eat meat.* Photo by Michelle Reddy

45

How do polar bears catch seals?

Polar bears spend much of their lives on ice floes—large, flat pieces of floating ice. This is where they hunt ringed seals.

Polar bears don't catch seals in the water. Instead, they sit and wait for seals to haul out where the ice and open water meet, or at holes in the ice where seals come up to breathe.

They also stalk seals sunning themselves on the ice and break into seals' birthing dens in snowdrifts to get newborn pups.

▼ *Polar bears almost always eat only meat. They feed mainly on ringed seals (shown here) and bearded seals.*

▲ *Arctic foxes often follow polar bears to scavenge leftover food from the bear's kill. If it were not for polar bears' hunting success, many foxes would not survive.*

▼ *One way polar bears catch seals is by swimming along the ice edge. The bear dives and swims underwater between holes in the ice until it is next to the seal lying on the ice. Then the bear attacks the seal.*

Photo by Brendan P. Kelly

46

Is it true that a polar bear covers the nose during hunting?

Some people think a polar bear covers its black nose with its white paw when sneaking up on prey. That way, the polar bear won't be seen.

But this is just a tall tale. Scientists have never seen a polar bear do this.

▲ *Bear cubs stay close to their mother while she looks for food. This keeps them safe and also helps cubs learn how to find food for themselves.*

▲ *Polar bears and brown bears scavenge carcasses of stranded whales.*

This brown bear is sitting on a dead gray whale.

▶ *It might surprise you to see this brown bear grazing on grass. The bear almost looks like a cow.*

What do brown bears eat?

What brown bears eat depends on where they live, the time of year, and the food available.

Berries, grasses, nuts, and roots make up about 75% of the bear's diet. Brown bears feed on more than 200 plant types.

The rest of the diet includes fish, insects, mammals, and honey.

47

▼ ▲ *Above and below.* *Bears locate ant nests by looking for decaying logs and tree stumps. The bear then uses smell to figure out where to break into the ant nest.*

▲ *Bears slurp and gulp water, while dogs and cats lap at water. How much water a bear drinks during the day depends on the bear species, the weather, and what the bear is doing.*

▼ *Insects, like these yellow ants, are high in protein and fat.*

Do brown bears kill large animals for food?

Brown bears rarely kill hoofed animals that are large, full-grown, and healthy. They sometimes kill young, small elk, deer, and moose.

Bears do eat carcasses of animals that have died, especially moose that has been winter- or wolf-killed.

Photo by Chet Hickox

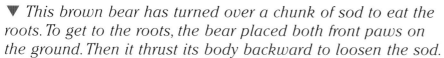

▼ *This brown bear has turned over a chunk of sod to eat the roots. To get to the roots, the bear placed both front paws on the ground. Then it thrust its body backward to loosen the sod.*

Photo by Pieter Folkens

◀ *Brown bears can run down moose and caribou.*
Bears need to be careful with moose, since this animal could kick the bear in the head and seriously hurt it.

Photo by Pieter Folkens

▲ *After eating its fill, a brown bear usually hides its meal by covering it with dirt and leaves. Then the bear can go away and return later to eat more.*
This is called a cache *(pronounced "CASH"). This is a brown bear's cache of caribou.*

49

► *Acorns and other nuts provide black bears with a good source of fats and proteins.*

Bear biologists call nuts "hard mast."

What do black bears eat?

Black bears are not picky about what they eat. What a bear eats depends on where the bear lives and what time of year it is.

Black bears eat a wide variety of food, including berries, nuts, grasses, new leaves, insects, and a small amount of meat. They scavenge meat from animal carcasses. In spring, they also prey on newborn deer and even moose. If a bear lives near a good fishing area, it won't pass up a good fish dinner.

Black bears eat honey when they find it, and unfortunately, they also feed in unfenced garbage dumps.

▲ *In spring and summer, black bears eat pawpaw and other fruit.*

▲ *Fruits, like these raspberries, are full of sugars and carbohydrates.*

Fruits are "soft mast."

▲ *Spectacled bears in South America eat prickly-pear cactus. American black bears also eat it in the Southwest.*

50

What do sun bears eat?

Sun bears eat fruit, small rodents, lizards, birds, insects (like ants and termites), and earthworms. They also enjoy honey and the hearts of coconut palm trees.

▲ *Sun bears search on the jungle floor and climb trees for food. They eat pretty much anything they can find.*

▶ *Spectacled bears eat figs while sitting in a tree.*
If you look closely, you can see bite marks from bears on some figs.

What do bears in South America eat?

Bromeliads make up half of the spectacled bears' diet. Spectacled bears also feed on unopened palm leaves, palm nuts, cactus, and fruits, but they eat meat if they can find it.

▶ *Some bromeliads can be tough to eat, so few animals will eat them.*
To eat this bromeliad, a spectacled bear would strip away the spiny leaves, much like we would when eating an artichoke.

How do giant pandas eat bamboo?

Giant pandas sit while eating. These bears have a sixth toe that is like your thumb; it helps the panda hold bamboo stems.

Giant pandas prefer thick bamboo shoots, and in 37 seconds, they can strip away the hard bark and eat the soft, juicy inside. Bamboo is not very digestible. Giant pandas spend over 13 hours a day eating to get enough to eat.

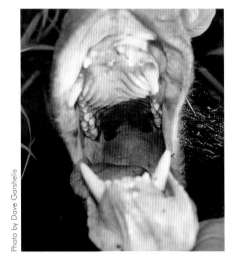

What do sloth bears like to eat?

Sloth bears feed on termites and ants, which they noisily suck up, using the snout like a vacuum. Sloth bears sometimes also scavenge tiger kills if they get a chance.

◀ The sloth bear has a big palate (roof of the mouth) and a really long tongue. It doesn't have two incisors (front teeth).

To suck up a meal of termites and ants, the bear makes a tube with its flexible lips and tongue. The bear first puffs out to blow away dirt. Then it closes its nostrils and vacuums up the insects with its mouth.

The noise a sloth bear makes while eating can be heard up to 330 feet (100 m) away.

▲ *Sloth bears are specially adapted for feeding on insects. They have a long, hairless snout and long, 3-inch (8-cm), curved claws to dig into hard termite mounds.*

▲ *Termite mounds often measure 3½ to 6½ feet (1–2 m) tall.*

How do bears find food?

Bears rely on their sense of smell to find food.

Grizzlies can smell rotting carcasses or garbage up to 2 miles (3.2 km) away!

▲ *Our garbage is full of smells and tasty food that tempt bears like this black bear.*

▲ *Bears can greatly damage trees when they tear off pieces of bark to get the sap inside.*
A nursing female spectacled bear tore up this tree. The sweet sap is high in calories and gives the bear energy.

Do bears ever steal food?

If given a chance, bears steal food from each other and from other animals. If they find it, bears will even take your picnic lunch.

When fishing, bears might try to steal each other's fish and sometimes have a tug-of-war. If bears find leftovers of another animal's kill, they usually try to scavenge them.

Bears even search for nuts and acorns hidden by small rodents and birds.

When do bears eat?

Most bears look for and eat food in the daylight. Sloth bears and desert spectacled bears, which live in hot climates, find food in the cooler night.

◀ *In spring, brown bears and American black bears use their keen sense of smell, as well as sight, to hunt fawns and newborn moose.*

▼ *This page. In Alaska, for 6 weeks in summer, salmon swim from the ocean upstream to spawn, and brown bears eat as many fish as they can catch.*

On a good day, a bear catches over 20 salmon. The fish weigh about 6 pounds (3 kg) each. One bear caught 69 salmon in one day!

Each brown bear uses its own fishing methods. Some pin the fish to the bottom, some grab the fish, and others wait along rapids to nab jumping fish right out of the air. Still others scoop fish out of the water with a sweep of the paws.

Photo by Hans-Joachim Muench

▲ *When first catching fish, a hungry bear eats whatever it catches. As the bear becomes less hungry, it eats female fish. Later, it prefers fish eggs, or roe.*

When bears do this, they leave the remaining fish for other bears, birds, and animals to scavenge.

Photo by Hans-Joachim Muench

Photos by Hans-Joachim Muench

54

Do bears really eat tree bark?

Brown, spectacled, Asiatic black, and American black bears grab tree bark with their teeth and tear off pieces.

These bears are really interested in the inner bark (cambium layers) and sap, because of the sweet taste. This is bad for the trees.

Do bears get fat?

Absolutely! On a good summer day, bears eat about 30 pounds (14 kg) of food.

When bears are getting ready for hibernation, they go on an eating binge just before retreating to their dens. They may triple the amount of food they eat.

Bears that live near landfills or cornfields get very fat and may even double their normal weight.

▶ *Like all bears before hibernating, this brown bear eats constantly to build up a thick layer of fat. Bears pluck the berries with their lips.*

Photo by International Fund for Animal Welfare, Chris Davis

▲ *Asiatic black bears feed on fruit and nuts still on the tree. To eat acorns, the bear plucks the acorn with its lips, peels it with its teeth, spits out the shell, and eats the kernel.*

In a day, one bear can eat as much as 11 pounds (5 kg). That means it has peeled about 4,000 to 12,000 acorns. (About 1,000 acorns are in a pound.)

Do bears build nests when feeding?

Spectacled bears usually bend back branches so that the tree branches holding fruit can also hold the bear's weight. The pile of branches is about 4 feet (1.2 m) across and can look like a nest.

Asiatic black bears sometimes build "nests," too. In Japan, a "nest" is a sign that these bears were feeding.

What does an Asiatic black bear eat?

Depending on the time of year and what food is available, Asiatic black bears may eat acorns, bamboo, nuts, berries, fruit, and insects. They also scavenge meat if they can find it.

Photo by Carol Fairfield, courtesy of Bill Lang

BEAR REPRODUCTION

Bears are mammals, so they produce live babies that nurse milk from their moms. Bear milk is very rich and thick, more like whipping cream.

Baby bears are helpless at birth and, like humans, they are totally dependent on their mothers for survival.

Little is known about reproduction in Asiatic black bears, spectacled bears, or sun bears.

Photo by Grady Baxter

▲ *This giant panda cub, Hua Mei, is less than a year old and lives in the San Diego Zoo. Zoos help protect endangered species.*

What do bears and pigs have in common?

Adult male bears and pigs are called boars. Both female adult bears and pigs are called sows. However, these two species are not related.

◀ *Opposite page. Bear moms put a lot of time and energy into raising their young. This is a polar bear mom with her cub.*
Photo by Chicago Zoological Society, Jim Schulz

Photo by Chicago Zoological Society, Howard Greenblatt

Then what are baby bears called?

Baby bears are generally called cubs. In its first year of life, a bear cub is called a coy (rhymes with *boy*); that's short for "cub of the year."

◀ *Here is a spectacled bear sow with her young cub.*

How old does a female have to be to have cubs?

Many bears reach sexual maturity between the ages of 3 and 8 years, but it depends on the species. The age bears begin to have cubs also depends on food availability, nutrition, and habitat.

So how do mates find each other for breeding?

Generally, spring is time for breeding. Giant panda females attract mates by leaving scent marks from special glands. Polar bears and brown bears urinate often as a cue.

Males follow these scents and fight with each other for the female. Usually the biggest ones win. Female bears won't breed until they are ready, and courtship may take less than a day.

A female may breed with several males, so cubs born at the same time may have different fathers. Males often breed with several females, than go back to a solitary life. Female bears give birth and raise cubs on their own.

Photo by Chicago Zoological Society, Mike Greer

▲ *Once bears breed, they go their separate ways. The male bear does not help the mother bear raise the cubs.*

How do they mate?

When it is time for the female to breed, the male mounts her from the back and holds onto her with his front paws, very much like dogs. Depending on the species, breeding may last a few minutes (giant panda) to half an hour (polar bear).

How long after mating are the cubs born?

Pregnancy lasts about 3 to 5½ months for giant pandas, 3 to 3½ months for sun bears, 5½ to 8 months for spectacled bears, 6 to 7 months for sloth bears, and 6 to 9 months for polar bears, black bears, and brown bears.

Photo by Michelle Reddy

▲ *Males follow females until the female is ready to breed. This male spectacled bear is following a female.*

58

Why is there so much variation even within the same bear species?

Bears have something called *delayed implantation*. That is when the fertilized egg starts to grow but stops at an early stage of development.

Then the embryo or blastocyst just floats around for a while. When it gets a signal from the mother bear's body, it attaches (implants) itself to the womb inside the mother bear. That's when it can continue to grow into a baby bear.

No one knows for sure what the signal is. It could take a short time or a long time, and that explains the different pregnancy lengths.

If conditions are not right (like there is not enough food for the mom and her cubs), the signal may never come. If that happens, the mother bear will have to start all over the next year.

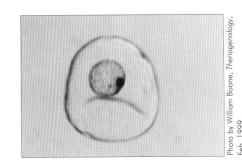

Photo by William Boone, *Theriogenology*, Feb. 1999

▲ *The bear blastocyst in this enlarged photograph is actually the size of a pinhead.*

Photo by Pieter Folkens

▲ *Brown bears give birth to one to four cubs, most often two.*

When and where are baby bears born?

It depends on the species. Polar bears, Asiatic black bears, American black bears, and brown bears have cubs during the coldest time of the year—a time when some bears go into dens for winter sleep. This is when the cubs are born.

Female polar bears use ice caves for dens, or they dig a den in the snow or ground. Many choose a den site that is on a hill so that they can watch for danger. Other species, like Asiatic black bears, give birth in hollow tree trunks or caves.

Even though the sloth bear, sun bear, and giant panda do not hibernate, they go into secluded dens to give birth.

Dens can be in caves, hollow trees, logs, or simply underground. Giant pandas use either a cave or a hollow tree lined with sapling branches. The mother bear stays in the den until her cub is about 30 days old.

What does a maternity den look like?

Each species creates a den that fits its needs. A typical maternity den for a polar bear is snug, with just enough room for mom and baby bears. Warmed by the mother's body heat, it can be much warmer inside the den than outside. The den is built with an upward slope, and because heat rises, the warmth stays inside.

The floors of dens may be covered with grasses, herbs, leaves, and branches. The mother's breath also helps keep the cubs warm.

Photo by Minnesota Department of Natural Resources, Dave Garshelis

▲ *Black bear moms give birth and begin nursing cubs while they are hibernating in their winter dens.*

Photo by Chicago Zoological Society, Jim Schulz

◀ *While in the den, mother bears consume the wastes from the cubs. This eliminates odors that might attract predators.*

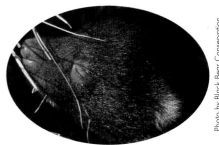

Photo by Black Bear Conservation Committee

▲ *Bear cubs are born helpless—unable to see, smell, hear, or walk. This black bear cub will be able to see when it is 28 to 40 days old.*

What do baby bears look like when they are born?

Even though adult bears are large, bears are very small when they are born. Black bears weigh less than half a pound (230 g), about the size of a kitten. At birth, a giant panda is about the size of a hamster, about 3½ ounces (100 g), nearly 1,000 times smaller than its mother.

Spectacled bear and sloth bear babies weigh 11 to 18 ounces (300–500 g), and polar bears weigh 1 pound (454 g) or less at birth.

They don't have any teeth, and their eyes don't open for a few weeks. Most bears are born without hair. Only polar bears and giant pandas are covered with thin white fur at birth.

▼ *This bear cub is just 1 to 2 months old.*

Photo by Randy Hadaway, *Theriogenology*, Feb. 1999

▲ *A polar bear cub nurses rich milk at one of its mother's six teats, or nipples.*

What do baby bears eat?

Bears are mammals. Like all mammals, the babies feed on rich milk that comes from their mothers. While they are nursing, cubs make a humming sound. Denning mother bears do not eat, so milk is produced from energy stored in the mother's body. It takes lots of energy to make milk.

Milk provides baby bears with nutrition and helps protect them from disease.

Like many bears, black bears produce milk that is 10 to 40% fat (compared to 3½% for humans). The young may nurse for 10 minutes every 2 to 3 hours. After feasting on their mother's rich milk for 2 months, polar bear cubs gain 30 to 40 pounds (14 to 18 kg).

A mother giant panda holds her cub like a human baby to nurse. Giant pandas nurse for 8 to 9 months, and sloth bears nurse cubs for 12 to 14 months.

▼ *Spectacled bear cubs are born during the rainy season. They come out of the den when fruits ripen.*

Photo by Chicago Zoological Society, Howard Greenblatt

How many bear cubs are born at one time?

Black bears usually produce a litter of two or three, and occasionally five, cubs every 2 years. Sloth and spectacled bears rarely have more than two cubs. Giant pandas give birth to one or two cubs, but usually only one survives. If the second cub survives, the mother will not have another cub for 2 years.

Polar bears can have a litter of one to three, but it takes a mature, experienced female to successfully raise all three. In a lifetime, a polar bear may only produce two litters.

Brown bears produce a litter of one to five cubs about every 3 years (four or five cubs is rare), but only half will reach adulthood.

Why don't all cubs survive?

Even a very protective mother bear cannot guard against all dangers. Falls, predators, adult male bears, diseases, and starvation could threaten cubs.

Photo of brown bear by Pieter Folkens

Do bear cubs like to play?

Yes, and play is very important for cubs. It prepares them for hunting, fighting, and knowing who and when not to fight. By playing, cubs become stronger and more coordinated, and they learn to think for themselves.

They also learn to read signals from other bears. When a polar bear wags its head from side to side, it is inviting another polar bear to play.

Playing may look like fighting, with pushing, biting, and swatting, but bears are very careful not to hurt each other.

Polar bears begin to play when still in the den, and they may even dig a special area for playing. But the real fun begins when they come out of the den and have lots of space for romping and snowy hills for sliding.

Cubs with no siblings, like giant pandas, play with mom or alone—rolling, climbing, and tumbling.

How do mother bears get food in the den?

Once the female gets settled in her den, she usually won't come out to eat until after the cubs are a few months old and the weather is warmer. Instead, the fat stored in her body provides the "food" and energy she needs to keep warm and to keep her body alive.

Photo by Chicago Zoological Society, Mike Greer

▲ *Cubs are careful not to hurt each other during play. If they get too rough, mom will correct them.*

▲ *Female bears are extremely attentive and protective of their cubs.*

Do bears lift their cubs by the scruff of the neck?

A mother bear moves young cubs by putting the cub's head in her mouth. Only the sloth bear is different.

After leaving the den, sloth bear moms give youngsters a piggyback ride for 6 to 7 months. The cubs won't even start to come down until they are about 3 months old. Cubs may stay on mom's back while she digs for termites.

Do bears go to school?

Bears are home-schooled. Some things, like climbing, come naturally. Giant panda and black bear cubs stay with their moms 1 to 1½ years. Brown bears stay for at least 2½ years, and sloth bears stay for 1½ to 2½ years. Sloth bear siblings stay together another 2 years.

During this time, cubs learn what to eat, where to find the best food, and how to deal with danger.

School's out when the cubs are old enough to be on their own. Mom chases them off before she breeds again.

Do bears make good pets?

People tend to like baby animals, especially if they look soft and cuddly. As babies, bear cubs can become very attached to humans if they are treated like pets.

But before long, cubs begin to treat people as they would a mother, sister, or brother bear. In other words, they begin to play rough. Because they are so strong and grow so fast, they can easily injure people and things.

Since bears are very curious, they can become a nuisance and be very destructive as they get bigger.

If you see a baby bear in the wild by itself, leave it alone (tell a park ranger later). The mother may be nearby and plan to return soon.

SELF-DEFENSE

Like all animals, bears protect themselves in their own way. If trying to escape or warn off an enemy doesn't work, bears might become aggressive. They can use sharp teeth and powerful claws.

Do bears get scared?

Bears can be frightened or surprised by something that they hear, smell, or see.

An adult bear that's startled usually takes a deep breath, and its ears prick up. A frightened cub flattens its ears, and its eyes get wide and roll.

◀ *Opposite page. Bears fight over food or when their space is invaded.*

Mothers trying to protect cubs, and two males interested in the same female, could fight.

Photo by Chicago Zoological Society, Mike Greer

How do bears protect themselves?

The first defense is to avoid danger. One way is to retreat. Bears flatten their ears and roar, or "chuff," to warn off enemies. They sometimes charge to scare off the animal. Mother bears often do this to defend their cubs.

To threaten another animal, a bear usually opens its mouth wide to display its large teeth. If the enemy doesn't leave, the bear decides whether to stay and fight or to run.

Different species make different decisions at this point. Black bears rarely attack when frightened, if an avenue of escape exists. Open-habitat species are more likely to attack.

Bears use brute strength to protect themselves—fighting tooth and nail. Their large teeth are a powerful weapon. Bears can strike crushing blows with their forepaws, using sharp claws to tear.

Young sloth bears, by gathering in small groups, may protect themselves against larger sloth bears or predators.

Photo of sloth bears by Chicago Zoological Society, Rick Search

How do moms protect their cubs?

It depends on the bear species. Big bear species, like polar bears or brown bears that live in wide, open spaces, try to protect their cubs by standing their ground and directly attacking the enemy.

Even a big male would think twice when faced with an angry mother bear protecting her cubs.

▲ *When cubs are afraid, they call out for their mothers. That's what this spectacled bear cub is doing.*

▼ *Bears communicate dominance, wanting to fight, and other information by how they move or hold the head.*

Black bear moms are smaller than brown bears. Since they live in forests, they often send cubs up a nearby tree and then run away. When danger is past, mom returns to her cubs.

Black bear moms encourage cubs to climb rough-bark trees, like pine, which are easier to climb than smooth-bark trees, like aspen.

▲ *Sharp claws are used by bears to protect themselves.*

▲ *Brown bear moms protect their cubs by standing their ground.*

66

Why do sloth bear moms carry cubs?

Cubs ride on the sloth bear mom's back. This helps the mom protect them against attacks by tigers, leopards, and other sloth bears.

Polar bear and spectacled bear cubs sometimes climb on the mother's back when danger threatens.

▲ *Although sloth bears are good climbers, they usually run from predators. Leopards, their chief predator, are also good at climbing trees.*

▼ *Black bear cubs climb trees when faced with danger. Polar bears live in places with no trees, so they rely on being aggressive to protect their cubs.*

◄ *Bears can use their large canines (fangs) to help protect themselves against enemies. Bears scare enemies by roaring with an open mouth (to show their teeth).*

If you look closely at the nose of this spectacled bear, you can imagine the damage that bear teeth can do.

Are hibernating bears able to protect themselves?

Bears that are hibernating wake up easily if disturbed. If a predator, such as a wolf, discovered the den, the bear would be able to defend itself.

Do bears ever kill each other?

Larger bears can kill smaller bears. Adult males may kill cubs. Adult male bears also sometimes kill females that protect cubs or young males that challenge them.

An adult male bear could even attack a young male minding his own business.

First, the older bear tries to scare the younger one into leaving. If he refuses, the younger bear stands a good chance of being killed.

One bear species may also kill another bear species. Brown bears sometimes kill black bears, for instance. When brown and black bears live in the same region, black bears stay in forests.

Do polar bears have enemies?

Polar bears, like grizzlies, really don't have any enemies, except people and maybe each other.

▲ *Polar bear cubs are sometimes killed by adult males.*

▲ *These are the remains of a young bear that was eaten by another bear.*

◀ *Brown bears sometimes attack and kill smaller relatives—American and Asiatic black bears.*

▲ *A walrus, with its long tusks, can seriously injure a polar bear trying to kill it.*

Do big cats kill bears?

Tigers, mountain lions, jaguars, and leopards sometimes fight and kill bears. Mountain lions and bobcats may kill young bear cubs.

▲ *Tigers sometimes kill Asiatic black bears, sloth bears, and sun bears.*

Do any wild dogs ever bother bears?

Wild Asiatic dogs, wolves, and even domestic dogs may interact with bears. The outcome usually depends on how big the bear is and how many dogs there are.

▲ *Single wolves often run when they see an adult bear, but they sometimes kill cubs. A pack of wolves can kill even a full-grown black bear.*

Brown bears and wolves usually don't pay much attention to each other, but there are reports of black bears being killed in their winter dens by wolves. A bear warns off a wolf by slapping its paw on the ground.

Do bear cubs have any enemies?

Yes, bear cubs, like other young animals, face many dangers.

Eagles, wolves, big cats, and adult male bears of their own and other species threaten them. However, the biggest danger for bear cubs, like that for adult bears, is people.

Photo of black bear by Pieter Folkens

69

BEARS AND PEOPLE

Bears have fascinated people throughout history. In many cultures, bears connect people with nature. Bears have been worshipped but hunted, loved yet feared.

What threats do bears face? How do people study bears?

▲ *Injuries to people from black bears usually result from bears' associating people with food. Sometimes people hand-feed bears on roadsides. Bears, looking for food, try to break into parked cars.*

▲ *The spectacled bear has deep roots in the myths and history of Andean cultures. Depending on the area, the bear is revered as a god or considered evil and killed.*

Are bears important to nature?

Every living thing is important to the Earth's healthy eco-systems. Like other animals, bears disperse seeds by eating fruit and berries.

Grizzlies also act as gardeners. In subalpine meadows, they dig and feed on bulbs of glacier lilies. When bears rake up the soil, they increase the nitrogen in the soil. That helps more plants grow in that area.

Because bears are at the top of the food chain, they help show us how healthy their environment is.

Scientists have found pollutants in polar bears. These pollutants, they discovered, have come to the Arctic up through the atmosphere and the world's oceans.

◄ *Opposite page.* *Female brown bears with cubs can be extremely dangerous to people.*

Photo by Pieter Folkens

71

Are any bears endangered?

All bear populations in the world today are smaller than they once were. Bears are found in fewer places than they were in earlier centuries. The most endangered bears live in Asia. Giant pandas, sloth bears, sun bears, and Asiatic black bears face the greatest threats.

Polar bears and American black bears have the most stable populations of all bear species.

▶ *Logging can destroy a bear's habitat. Roads that help people get logs to market may also bring hunters and poachers who kill bears. Roads also disrupt bears' natural travel routes.*

Bears do not feed in clearcut lands with no food trees, like oaks, or cover to hide in. Harvesting trees can displace bears and force them to live closer to people. That can create conflicts.

That's why it's important to manage logging activities carefully.

▲ *Bears that damage bee yards can cost beekeepers hundreds of dollars. Barriers such as electric fences can help keep bears from harming gardens, small fields, and beehives.*

Photo by Reno P. Sommerhalder

What kind of human threats do bears face?

Bears compete with people for space and food. People cut down trees and use land for growing crops and grazing livestock. This means that bears lose places where they live—their habitat. This also means that bears come into contact more with people.

▼ *Bears sometimes raid crops, like sugarcane, that grow near where they live. Farmers do not like this, and a few kill bears for destroying their crops.*

Photo by Dagmar C. Fertl

Photo by Black Bear Conservation Committee, Paul Davidson

Photo by Bill Long

▲ *In places where bear species are not threatened, some bears are legally hunted. Governments regulate bear hunting, which can help control the number of bears in an area and get rid of problem bears. With hunting managed carefully, American black bear populations actually increase.*

Photo by Bernie Peyton

Photo by Bernie Peyton

Why do people hunt and kill bears?

People kill bears for many reasons. Some bears are killed for food. Thousands of American black bears are eaten each year.

Other bears are hunted for their pelts. Still others are shot because they destroy crops or beehives or go through garbage dumps and rummage for food at camp-sites. Ranchers sometimes kill bears that feed on their sheep and cattle. Some bears may be killed simply because people fear them.

Bile from bear gallbladders is used in traditional Chinese medicine. Also, bear paws are considered a delicacy in Chinese cuisine.

◀ *Two photos left.* *Clearing land destroys habitats that help bears survive.*

This slash-and-burn field was chopped out of a cloud forest in the Cayambe-Coca Ecological Reserve in Ecuador. In the dry season, people burn the field. Then they plant corn, beans, and squash.

73

People have also used bears in traditional spiritual ceremonies. People still kill them today for sports trophies or in self-defense.

What is poaching?

Poaching means illegally killing animals that laws protect. Poachers who kill bears hide their activities from authorities. That's because they can make a lot of money from buying and selling bear parts.

Photo by Michelle Reddy

▲ *Poaching is a serious threat to giant pandas.*
In the 1980s, poachers could make $3,000 or more for a pelt. These pelts were resold for over $10,000.

Photo by Adolph Murie

▲ *Russia has the largest brown bear population in the world. Brown bears once ranged throughout Europe. People killed them for sport and because they sometimes attack livestock.*
Small populations of brown bears now live scattered throughout Eurasia.

Are bears killed in other ways?

Yes. Bears that try to cross busy roads or railroad tracks are sometimes hit by cars or trains. Some also die accidentally by climbing poles with electrical wiring.

Is global warming affecting bears?

Warmer temperatures means less ice in the Arctic. Some people think that changes in Arctic ice conditions might be why Canadian polar bears are growing thinner and having fewer cubs.

Ice is important to polar bears. They use ice floes as a platform from which to hunt the seals they eat. During summer, near Hudson Bay in Canada, the ice melts, and polar bears are forced to live on land. Since food is not as easy for them to find in summer, the bears fast.

Global warming would increase the time that polar bears fast. Also bears and people may have more conflicts if polar bears spend more time on land.

Do bears have to worry about pollution?

Bears, like other animals and plants, are exposed to many types of pollution—plastics, chemicals, noise, oil, and contaminants in their environment.

Bears that feed in garbage dumps are not finicky eaters. They sometimes get tangled up in plastic. Other bears accidentally eat plastic. Toxic chemicals have been found in bear tissue. Bears that live near farms are directly exposed to pesticides.

Polar bears feed on seals that have pollutants concentrated in their thick fat or oil on their fur. When polar bears groom themselves, they could also ingest oil from their fur. Nursing mother bears could pass these pollutants on to cubs. Also, some polar bears develop reproductive problems from pollutants.

Although bears can be disturbed by people's noise, they tend to tolerate it. Airplanes, machinery, snowmobiles, and oil drilling now surround many bear populations.

Photo by Dagmar C. Fertl

◀ *When U.S. President Theodore ("Teddy") Roosevelt went on a hunting trip, he refused to shoot a black bear cub. A cartoon featured the event, and soon stuffed toy manufacturers popularized "Teddy's bear."*
This jointed Steiff bear is made in Germany.

Photo by International Fund for Animal Welfare

▲ *These polar bears, found eating garbage in town, are considered a nuisance. People move the bears to keep them out of trouble. Since bears may simply return to their original habitat, this usually isn't very successful.*

If I wanted to study bears, what would I be?

People with lots of different specialties—like biologists, zoologists, veterinarians, and mammalogists—often work as a team to learn about bears and how to save them.

How do you catch a wild bear?

Very carefully. First scientists lure the bear into a safe place. Then they give the bear something to make it sleepy. Then they weigh, measure, and tag the bear.

This does not hurt the bear.

How do you follow a wild bear?

A bears can be fitted with a radio collar. The collar sends out signals that are picked up by special radio receivers. This allows people to track the bear's movements.

This helps people understand how bears live and where they go.

▲ *Before scientists can put a tag or radio collar on a bear, they need to catch the bear.*
They use baited barrels, like this one, to safely catch bears.

▲ *This sedated black bear is getting a radio collar.*
A bandana protects the bear's eyes since the drug makes the bear unable to blink for a short time.

▲ *Scientists are weighing this bear. It would be hard to weigh a bear that was awake!*
They gave the bear something to put it in a deep sleep while they were handling it.

76

▲ *Scientists can locate a bear with a radio collar by using an antenna on the ground, on a plane, or even from a satellite.*

▲ *This 3-pound (1.4-kg) black bear cub is being relocated with its mother and fellow cub(s) to a new home.*

Why do people move bears from one place to another?

People move bears to reintroduce them in places where they no longer live. They also move pregnant female bears or mother bears with cubs to new places. This helps conserve bears.

Sometimes they move nuisance bears—bears that get into trash and bother people—to other areas.

▲ *This black bear has a tag in its ear and a radio collar around its neck. The tag helps scientists identify the individual bear.*
The collar has a small radio-tracking device that helps them find the bear and learn about where bears go and what they do.

▲ *This orphan bear cub was rehabilitated and released into the wild. This can be hard because cubs become attached to people.*
It makes them less wary of people, which can spell trouble.

77

Do bears attack people?

Like any wild animal, bears may attack people. Bears seldom do this, but they can hurt you quite badly if it happens. Female bears with cubs that feel threatened may attack. Male bears are responsible for most serious American black bear attacks.

In a national park, people are 100 times more likely to have a car accident than to be attacked by a bear.

▲ *Bears are curious about their environment. These black bear cubs look as though they're trying to figure out how to break into this car.*

What can we do to help bears?

Both bears and people live on Earth, so people have to learn how to be good neighbors. Everyone can do something to help. We need to be more tolerant and understanding of bears' needs.

For example, instead of destroying bears' habitats, we can work together to protect them. In some places, people are building wildlife tunnels under roads or passageways over roads to keep bears safe from traffic.

▲ *Zoos help preserve endangered species, like this giant panda. Only about 1,000 giant pandas remain in the wild today.*

In other places, people have kept forest corridors between farmlands to help bears safely travel from place to place.

Many zoos all over the world help by using a computerized "dating service" to match bears for breeding.

Preserves and sanctuaries give bears safe homes in the wild and strong laws control or stop the sale of bear products.

Photo by Dagmar C. Fertl

▲ *Forest corridors between farmlands help American black bears move from place to place unseen. They also keep bears from invading farms.*

What can kids do to help bears?

You help bears and other wildlife every time you recycle or conserve energy.

You have even helped bears just by reading this book and learning about them.

Now, share what you have learned with your family, friends, and classmates so they can help bears, too!

ACKNOWLEDGMENTS

We are grateful to the many photographers who were kind enough to provide photographs for this book: Bill Applegate; Grady Baxter; Dr. Judy Chupasko; Pam Coy; Richard Ellis; Wesley Elsberry; Carol Fairfield; Pieter Folkens; Dr. Dave Garshelis; Dr. Chet Hickox; Deborah Jefferson; Dr. Brendan Kelly; Hans-Joachim Muench; Dr. Bill Lang; Dr. Jan Murie for allowing us to use Dr. Adolph Murie's photos; Karen Noyce; Dr. Todd M. O'Hara; Dr. Bernie Peyton; the late Irene C. Rathburn; Cliff Rice; Dr. Naomi Rose; Dr. Dana Seagars; Monty Sloan; Reno P. Sommerhalder; Ingrid Visser; Jennifer Warmbold; Dave Winthrow; Dr. Victoria Woshner; Dr. Bernd Würsig; and Dr. Zhigang Jiang.

Dr. Melinda Pruitt-Jones made Chicago Zoological Society (CZS) photographs available; Nancy Pajeau helped pick out and duplicate needed CZS photos. CZS photographers include Erica Benson, Cynthia Fandl, Howard Greenblatt, Mike Greer, Rick Search, and Jim Schulz.

We also thank R. Riewe of the American Society of Mammalogists; Dr. William R. Boone and Dr. Randy Hadaway of the Center for Women's Medicine; Ami Culshaw and Chris Davis with the International Fund for Animal Welfare; Paul Davidson with the Black Bear Conservation Committee; Jean Fierke and Paul Friedrich of the Michigan Department of Natural Resources; Camila Fox for Diane Wilson at Animal Protection Institute; Dr. Daniel Koon and Thomas W. Budd at St. Lawrence University; Dr. Jill Robinson with the International Fund for Animal Welfare and Animal Asia Foundation. We also thank the *Theriogenology* journal for the use of previously published photographs.

We would like to thank Karen Noyce with the Minnesota Department of Natural Resources; Dr. Bernie Peyton with the International Union for the Conservation of Nature (IUCN) Bear Specialist Group; Reno P. Somerhalder with The BEAR Society; and Paul Davidson with the Black Bear Conservation Committee for patiently answering all of our

questions and reviewing the manuscript.

In addition, we thank Bill Applegate, Dr. Raymond Tarpley, and Josh Rosenberg for helping us locate photographs and information and Dr. Barbara Durrant for being a helpful resource for reproduction information. A very special thanks to Don Hoffman for emergency computer support, without whom we would not have met our deadline.

We especially thank Debra Skaar's 4th grade class at Lindbergh-Schweitzer Elementary School in San Diego, Simone Deslarzes, Dr. Ken Deslarzes, Sawyer Harrison, and Emily Morgan for helping us ask great questions about bears.

We are grateful to Tania Fertl for drawing the panda wrist and to Michelle V. Morin for creating the map of bear locations, based on the IUCN Bear Action Plan.

A very special note of thanks to Dr. Jeanette Green, our editor at Sterling, for her patience and gentle editing skills.

Last, but certainly not least, we thank our friends and families for their support.

INDEX

acorns, 55
activity, day–night, 20, 26–27, 53, 54
age, 23, 58
American black bear (*Ursus americanus*), 8–9, 14–16, 18, 24–26, 37, 40–41, 45, 48, 50, 53, 55, 60–63, 66–69, 75–78
ancestors of bears, 5, 13, 23
  origin, 5, 15
animal kingdom, 12–13
arctic foxes, 46
Asiatic black bear (*Ursus thibetanus*), 9, 15, 19, 25, 26, 37, 40, 55, 57, 59, 68–69, 72
  moon bear, 9
bear, most common, 18
beehives, 72, 73
biting, 23
black bears; *see* American black bear *and* Asiatic black bear
boar and sow, 57
body, 28–37
  adaptations, 29
  appearance, 5–11, 28–37
  color and markings, 5–11
  fat, 30, 55, 62
  fur (coat), 27, 29, 31–32, 42, 61
  size (weight), 5–11, 29, 55
boss (dominance), 21, 27, 66–69
brown bear (*Ursus arctos*), 4–5, 6–9, 13, 15–16, 18, 22, 25–30, 33, 37–39, 45, 47–49, 53–55, 58–59, 62–63, 66, 68, 69, 71, 74
  Alaskan Kodiak, 6, 25
  grizzly, 6–7, 22, 27, 53, 68, 71
  Kermode (spirit or ghost), 9
cache, 49
cactus, 22, 50, 51
Canidae family, 5
carcasses, 47, 49, 50
carnassial teeth, 33
carnivore (order Carnivora), 5, 13, 33
cats, big, 52, 67, 69
Chinese medicine and cuisine, 73
Chordata (phylum), 12–13
claws /clawing, 23, 34–35, 52, 65, 66
climbing trees, 29, 37, 51, 65-67
cloud forest, 15
communication, 22-23, 66
coy (cub), 57
cubs, 20, 21, 26–27, 47, 56–63, 66–69, 78
  father's role, 58
  frightened, 65–66
  as pets, 63

cubs (*cont.*)
  play-fighting, 21, 62–63
  protection and schooling (mom's role), 21, 47, 56–63, 65, 66–69
deer (caribou, elk, etc.) 49, 50, 53
den, 15, 24–25, 59–62
dog family, 5, 23
eagles, 69
ear(s) (pinnae), 39–41
ear tags, 76–77
ecosystems, 71
endangered bears, 19, 57, 72, 78
enemies, 27, 60, 62, 65–69
extinction, 13, 23
eyes (vision), 39, 41–42, 60
  third eyelid, 41–42
farms, 72, 73, 75, 79
fighting, 21, 26, 35, 65–69
fishing, 34, 47, 50, 53, 54
food (diet), 20–21, 25, 26–27, 30–31, 44–55, 61, 62, 63, 71, 73
  chain, 71
  eating habits, 33, 44–55
  fruit and nuts, 50–51, 53, 55
  hard and soft mast, 50
  land animals, 49–53
  plants, 33, 36, 49–52, 55
forest corridors, 78
fur (coat), 22, 27, 29, 31–32, 42, 61
  shedding, 22
garbage (trash), 20, 26–27, 45, 51, 53, 73, 75, 77
gardeners, bear, 71
genus, 12–13
giant panda (*Ailuropoda melanoleuca*), 10–11, 19, 33, 36–37, 39, 42, 44–45, 52, 57–58, 60–63, 72, 74, 78
  bamboo eater, 33, 36, 44–45, 52
  Hua Mei, 57
  raccoon not relative, 11
  wrist bone, 36
global warming, 74
Great Bear (Ursa Major), 5
grizzly, 6–7, 8, 22, 27, 53, 68, 71; *also see* brown bear
grooming, 27, 31
ground squirrels, 30
habitats; 5, 15–19
  how live, 29 14–27, 29, 71–79
hearing, 39, 40, 60
hibernation, 30–31, 60
honey, 11, 47, 50, 72
hunters and poachers, 27, 71–74
intelligence, 27, 63, 78

insects, 26, 31–32, 45, 47, 48, 50–52, 55
kids, how they can help, 79
koala bear (not a bear), 12
live, how bears, 14–27, 29, 54, 71–79
  groups or alone, 15, 20, 54
locations, bear, 15–19, 23, 68, 71–79
  map, 16
logging, 72
mammals, 13, 23, 47, 57
marking trees, path, 21, 22, 39, 58
marsupials, 12
medicine, 73, 76
miacids, 23
moose, 49, 50, 53
mouth (lips), 32
"nests," 55
Oligocene epoch, 23
omnivore(s), 32, 45
panda; *see* giant panda
paws (feet), 34–35, 36–37, 43
penguins, 17
people and bears, 27, 63, 71–79
  dangers, 63, 71, 78
pigs (boar and sow), 57
plantigrade, 35, 36
play-fighting, 21, 62, 63
poachers, 74
polar bear (*Ursus martimus*), 5, 15–17, 20–21, 27, 30–32, 35, 37, 39, 41, 43, 45–47, 56–62, 66–68, 71
  fur (coat hairs), 5–6, 27, 31, 32, 61
  marine mammal, 5
  nose and skin, 5, 32, 47
  swimming, 37, 41
pollution, 71, 75
populations, 72, 74
predators
  bears as, 32, 46–47, 49, 67, 68, 69
  enemies, 27, 60, 62, 65, 67–69
preserves/ sanctuaries, 73, 78–79
radio collar, 76–77
relocation, 77
reproduction, 56–63
  birth, 25, 32, 57–62
  blastocyst, 59
  breeding and mates, 27, 39, 58, 79
  delayed implantation, 59
  maturity, 58
  milk and nursing, 57, 61–62
  pregnancy, 58–62
running, 29, 34, 37
salmon, 6, 20, 27, 54
scavenging, 45, 46, 47, 49, 50, 52, 53, 54, 55
scratching, 38–39

scent (odors), 22, 58, 60
scientific classification, 12–13
scientists, 71, 76–77
seals and sea lions, 23, 27, 39, 45, 46
self-defense, 21, 33, 34, 63, 64–69
senses, 21, 38–43, 60
sight (vision), 39, 41, 42, 60
  third eyelid, 41–42
size, 5–11, 29; *also see* weight
skin, 5, 32, 42–43
sleep, 26, 30, 59; *also see* hibernation
sloth bear (*Melursus ursinus*), 10, 16, 19, 25, 31, 37, 40, 42, 52–53, 58, 61–63, 65, 67, 69
  piggyback ride, 63, 67
  snout, tongue, lips, 52
smell and nose, 21, 39, 41, 42, 43, 47, 52, 60
sounds, bear, 22, 23, 61, 65, 67
species, bear, 5–13, 23, 29
spectacled bear (*Tremarctos ornatus*), 7–8, 13, 15, 22, 26, 30, 35, 36, 37, 50–51, 53, 55, 57–58, 61–62, 66, 67, 71
  in Andean cultures, 71
  eye-ring pattern, 7–8
  standing, 21, 33
strength, 33, 63, 65
sun bear (*Helarctos malayanus*), 11, 15–16, 25, 31, 40, 42, 51, 57–58, 60, 72
  honey bear, 11
swimming, 29, 35, 37, 41
taste, 42
teddy bear (Roosevelt), 75
teeth, 23, 32–33, 61, 65, 67
  layers and age, 23
termites, 51, 52, 63
territory (range), 22, 26–27
touch, 38–39, 42–43
tongue, 42, 52
tree sap, 53, 55
Ursidae (bear family), 12–13
whiskers, 43
walking, 34–37, 60
walrus, 23, 45, 68
water, 26, 28–29, 48
weight (size), 5–11, 29, 55, 60, 61
whales, 47
winter (cold), 24, 25, 27, 29, 59, 62
wolves, 5, 49, 67, 69
zoo(s), 57, 78–79
  "dating service," 79